In The Wild

WHALES

Claire Robinson

Heinemann Library
Chicago, Illinois

Customer Service: 888-454-2279

Visit our website at www.heinemannlibrary.com

Designed by Celia Floyd
Illustrations by Alan Fraser (Pennant Illustration)
Printed and bound in Hong Kong/China by South China Printing Co.

05 04 03 02 01
10 9 8 7 6 5 4 3 2 1

Library of Congress Cataloging-in-Publication Data
Robinson, Claire, 1955-
    Whales / Claire Robinson.
        p. cm. – (In the wild
    Includes bibliographical references and index.
        Summary: Presents the physical characteristics, habitat,
    behavior, and life cycle of whales, with an emphasis on
    the humpback whale.
        ISBN 1-57572-865-6 (lib. bdg.)   ISBN 1-58810-325-0 (pbk. bdg.)
        1. Humpback whale—Juvenile literature.
    [1. Humpback whale. 2. Whales.] I. Title. II.
    Series: Robinson, Claire, 1955- In the wild.
    QL737.C424R639 1999
    599.5—dc21   98-34530
                                                                      CIP
                                                                      AC

Acknowledgments
The Publishers would like to thank the following for permission to reproduce photographs:
Ardea London Ltd./Francois Gohier, pp. 4 (left and right), p. 9, 11, 12-13, 18, 20, 22; Mike Osmond, p. 7, Jean-Paul Ferrero, p. 14; J.M La Roque, p. 17; Bruce Coleman/Mr. Johnny Johnson, p. 15; Natural History Unit/Doc White, pp. 8, 16, 19, 23; Oxford Scientific Films/Zig Leszczynsk, p .5 (left); Mark Newman, p. 5 (right); Ben Osborne, p. 6; C.J. Gilbert, p. 10; Duncan Murrell, p .21.

Cover photograph: Ardea/Francois Gohier.

Some words are shown in bold, **like this.** You can find out what they mean by looking in the glossary.

Contents

Whale Relatives

Whales are very large sea **mammals.** They don't have hair to keep them warm like most mammals. Instead, they have a thick layer of fat, called blubber.

grey whale

sperm whale

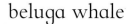
beluga whale

humpback whale

There are 75 kinds of whales. Humpbacks are one of the largest, growing longer than a large school bus. Let's see how they live.

Where Whales Live

Humpback whales live in every ocean. They spend most of their time in the **Arctic** Ocean and in water around **Antarctica.** These waters are icy.

Before winter comes, humpback whales **migrate** to warmer water. They will the spend the winter here with other whales.

Diving and Breathing

Whales swim by moving their tails up and down. Humpbacks have long flippers to help them turn and dive. They can stay underwater for 30 minutes between breaths.

This whale has come to the surface to breathe air. When whales breathe out through their **blowholes**, water on top of their head is blown upwards.

Finding Food

Humpbacks must eat a lot. The food they eat is very small. They eat tiny animals called krill. Krill look like small shrimp.

To catch krill, the whale swims to the water's surface with its mouth open. Its throat stretches wider as it fills up with krill.

Eating

Not all whales have teeth. Some whales have a **baleen** inside their mouth. A baleen traps krill inside, but lets water out.

These whales are feeding together. They
trap krill by blowing a net of bubbles. The
whales swim into the ring to eat the krill.

Migrating

Before winter comes, humpback whales **migrate** in groups. They swim thousands of miles to reach warmer water. Then they will **mate** and have babies

Humpbacks swim near the **coast**. They poke their heads above the surface to look around. Can you see this whale's eye?

Babies

The male humpback whale sings a strange and beautiful song. The song helps females to find him. The male and female dance and swim before they **mate**.

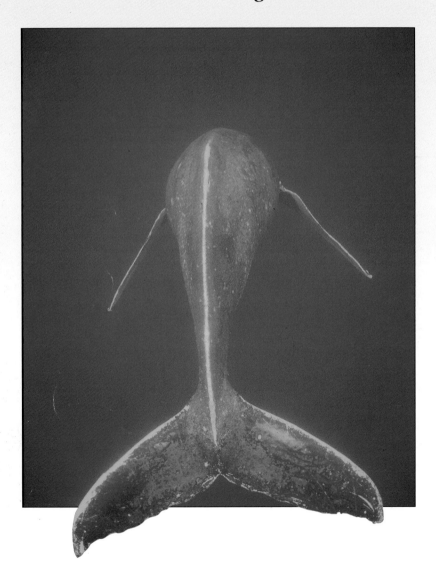

Eleven months after whales mate, a baby is born. Humpback whales give birth to one **calf**. Like other **mammals,** a whale calf drinks its mother's milk

Growing Up

The mother and **calf migrate** back to the cold waters in spring. The calf will stay close to his mother for one year.

As the calf grows, it will splash, dive, and leap in the air. This is how it learns to swim. It also learns how to find krill and how to blow net bubbles to trap them.

Whales and People

People used to hunt whales. Whale blubber was used to make oil and eaten as food. So many whales were killed that there are not many left now.

Today, people around the world are protecting whales. There are laws that stop people from hunting these gentle giants.

Humpback Whale Facts

- Whales are **mammals**; they feed their babies on milk and breathe air like humans.

- You can spot a humpback whale because of its humped back and the lumps on its head.

- Humpback whales can grow up to 62 feet (16 m) long.

- Humpback whales can live for up to 45 years.

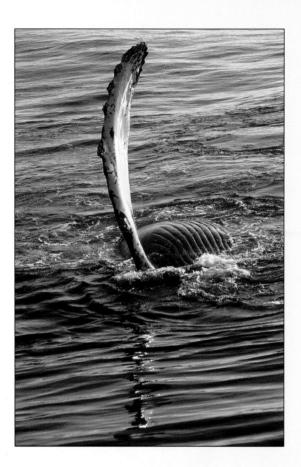

- Humpback whales are the only whales that sing songs. The songs can be heard many miles away through the water.

- Humpbacks have very long flippers that are white underneath and have lumpy edges.

- Humpback whales have no teeth. Instead, they separate their food through 350 layers of **baleen**.

Glossary

Antarctic   cold area around the South Pole

Arctic   cold area around the North Pole

baleen   teethlike layers in a whale's mouth that separate food from water

blowholes   nostrils on top of a whale's head

calf   baby whale

coast   land along the sea

mammals   warm-blooded animals that feed their babies milk made in the mother's body

mate   to find a partner to have babies with

migrate   to move from one place to another when seasons change

Index

More Books To Read

Cooper, Jason. *Whales of the Seas.* Vero Beach, Fla: Rourke, 1996.

Esbensen, Barbara J. *Baby Whales Drink Milk.* New York, NY: HarperCollins Children's Books, 1994.

Prevost, John F. *The Humpback Whale.* Minneapolis, Minn.: Abdo & Daughters Publishing, 1995.